TOTALLY
Silly
Science

STRANGE SPACE

by Robin Twiddy

BEARPORT
PUBLISHING

Minneapolis, Minnesota

CREDITS

Images are courtesy of Shutterstock.com. With thanks to Getty Images, Thinkstock Photo, and iStockphoto.

Recurring images – pics five (paper), Sonechko57 (splats), sebastian ignacio coll (explosion), MoonRock (texture), Ilija Erceg (eyes), Amy Li (illustrations). Cover – Sudowoodo, yatate, MicroOne, lexaarts. 2–3 – Tomsickova Tatyana, Nadya_Art. 4–5 – Alones, Andrei Verner, eaxx, Mooi Design, Oxy_gen. 6–7 – Aphelleon, Victoruler, Vadim Sadovski. 8–9 – gst, Gorodenkoff, Roman Samborskyi. 10–11 – Hvsht, Sudowoodo, GOLFX, Yakovlev Sergey. 12–13 – Ekaterina_Mikhaylova, Elena Shashkina, Frame Stock Footage. 14–15 – Thitisan, Aphelleon, solar22, Zakharchenko Anna. 16–17 – Dmitriy Nikiforov, canadianPhotographer56, KeyFame, rflyart, Stock Up. 18–19 – glenda, PremiumArt, eaxx. 20–21 – svtdesign, Gorodenkoff, WAYHOME studio, oljalja. 22–23 – vikas31, blocberry, Ilya Bolotov, maryna rodyukova. 24–25 – PremiumArt, NASA (wiki commons), HappyPictures, Maria Skrigan, Nadezda Barkova, wet nose. 26–27 – englishinbsas, Merlin74, Sira Anamwong. 28–29 – Nadya_Art, Alones, Milles Studio, eaxx. 30 – NikoNomad.

Library of Congress Cataloging-in-Publication Data is available at www.loc.gov or upon request from the publisher.

ISBN: 979-8-88822-019-1 (hardcover)
ISBN: 979-8-88822-207-2 (paperback)
ISBN: 979-8-88822-334-5 (ebook)

For more information, write to Bearport Publishing, 5357 Penn Avenue South, Minneapolis, MN 55419.

CONTENTS

SERIOUS SCIENCE

Science is always serious, right? Wrong! Science can be sillier than you might think.

Space is a very silly place. But there is some serious science behind it.

Get ready to enter the Silly Zone! Here, you will find all of the strangest things about space.

ANIMAL ASTRONAUTS

How did scientists first test their flights to space? They sent animals.

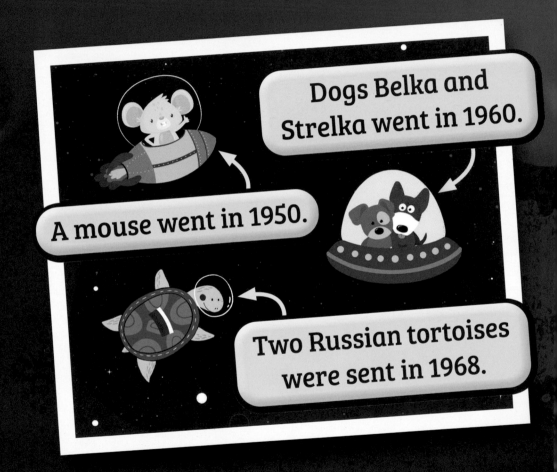

Dogs Belka and Strelka went in 1960.

A mouse went in 1950.

Two Russian tortoises were sent in 1968.

A surprising number of animals have been to space.

A chimpanzee named Ham is one of the most famous space animals. He was sent for a 16-minute spaceflight.

Ham's safe return proved space would be safe for human **astronauts**, too.

BODIES IN SPACE

Once we knew animals could make it to space and back, we sent people.

It turns out, human bodies won't change much after a few hours. However, some strange things might happen after a little bit longer.

On Earth, the liquid inside a human body is pulled down by **gravity**. There is no gravity in space. This means the liquid can go anywhere in the body.

Some astronauts get skinnier legs and puffier heads.

TALL TALES

Space makes astronauts taller, too.

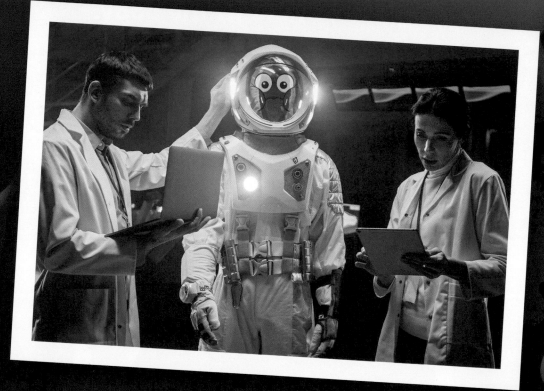

Astronauts arrive back on Earth about 3 **percent** taller than when they left!

But you don't have to go to space to grow. Just get a good night's sleep. You are always taller in the morning.

During the day, your body gets shorter as it is pulled down by gravity. It relaxes back to its full length at night.

SPACE TOILETS

Gravity also plays a big part in using a toilet. It helps pull waste down and away from you.

For years, astronauts didn't have toilets in space. They had to use little bags.

Astronauts got tired of using the bags. So, scientists solved the problem.

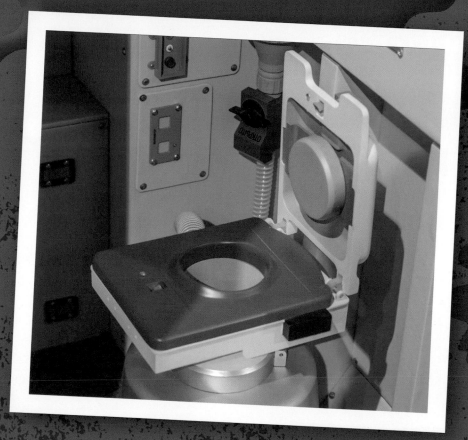

They came up with a toilet that sucks away poop so it doesn't float around.

NO SANDWICHES

Eating in space can be tricky, too. Loose crumbs could float into an astronaut's eyes or get stuck in the machinery.

In 1965, astronaut John Young smuggled a sandwich into space.

The sandwich started to break apart after only a few bites. Crumbs spread everywhere!

NASA banned bread in space.

Now, any food that makes crumbs isn't allowed in space. Other banned foods include fizzy drinks, salt, pepper, and fresh milk.

MOON GOLF

In 1971, Alan Shepard walked on the moon. There, he hit two golf balls. The balls traveled farther on the moon than they would have on **Earth**.

There is less gravity on the moon to slow things, such as golf balls, down.

However, Alan's spacesuit slowed his swing. He didn't break any records. On Earth, the farthest a golf ball had been hit was 787 yards (719 m).

Without heavy gear, a good golfer could probably hit the ball farther than 2 miles (3 km) on the moon.

SPACE CAR

There is a red electric sports car in space right now. A company called SpaceX sent it there to test their rockets.

They left the car in space with the radio playing music at full blast. But no one can hear it.

Space is a **vacuum**, so it has no air. Sound cannot travel without something to travel in.

Sound is made of **vibrations**. We hear it when the vibrations reach our ears.

DON'T CRY

Crying in space is harder than you might think!

When you cry on Earth, tears leave your eyes and roll down your cheeks. In space, tears build up into big balls of liquid around the eyes.

Without gravity, the tears float away when the wet balls get big enough.

Andrew Feustel was on a **spacewalk** when he started to tear up. The astronaut was stuck crying. You can't wipe your eyes when you're in a spacesuit!

BOILING TONGUES

People would not be able to survive in space without help from spacesuits, spacecraft, and space stations.

NASA scientist Jim LeBlanc found out what would happen to human bodies in space without spacesuits.

While running a test on Earth, Jim's spacesuit broke. The **saliva** on his tongue started bubbling and boiling. Luckily, he was quickly saved.

The liquids in your body would boil in a vacuum. Your body could double in size because of bubbles in your blood.

RAINING DIAMONDS

No one has ever been to Jupiter. The giant planet is made of mostly gas, so there would be nothing to stand on. But there may be something else.

Jupiter is covered in many powerful gas storms. Some scientists think the storms might rain diamonds!

They think the storms turn some gases into **carbon.**

Then, the carbon turns into diamonds as it falls from the storm.

JUMPING OVER THE MOON

Astronauts say walking without gravity is strange. What happens when they jump?

Gravity is six times stronger on Earth than it is on the moon. That means you could jump much higher on the moon!

On Earth, most people can jump about **12 inches (30 cm)** off the ground. The same jump on the moon would send you more than **9 feet (3 m)** high.

A kangaroo on the moon could jump more than 33 ft (**10 m**) high.

TOTALLY SILLY

From diamond rain to super-high jumps, space can be a pretty cool place.

Space has lots of silly science, too.

We learned that space toilets are made to suck away an astronaut's poop. And now we know why you shouldn't bring a sandwich into space.

Without silly science, we wouldn't know some really important things about space. And there is still so much to learn!

It looks like silly scientists + silly space = serious science! Sometimes, silly is important.

WHICH SPACE FACTS DO YOU THINK ARE THE SILLIEST?

GLOSSARY

astronauts people who travel into space

carbon an element common on many planets

gravity the force that pulls all things toward the ground

percent a part of a whole, shown as a number out of one hundred

saliva a clear liquid made in the mouth

smuggled secretly brought something

spacewalk going outside a spacecraft as an astronaut in space

vacuum without air or gas

vibrations quick back-and-forth shaking movements

INDEX

READ MORE

Finan, Catherine C. *Life in Space (X-treme Facts: Space).* Minneapolis: Bearport Publishing, 2022.

Keppeler, Eric. *More Freaky Space Stories (Freaky True Science).* New York: Gareth Stevens Publishing, 2020.

LEARN MORE ONLINE

1. Go to **www.factsurfer.com** or scan the QR code below.
2. Enter **"Strange Space"** into the search box.
3. Click on the cover of this book to see a list of websites.